# SCHIRMER'S LIBRARY
## OF MUSICAL CLASSICS

Vol. 434

# ALOYS SCHMITT

Op. 16

# Preparatory Exercises

(Five-Finger Exercises)

## For the Piano

NEW AND AUGMENTED EDITION

With Appendix by
A. KNECHT

ISBN 978-0-7935-2557-7

# G. SCHIRMER, Inc.

DISTRIBUTED BY

HAL•LEONARD®
CORPORATION
7777 W. BLUEMOUND RD. P.O. BOX 13819 MILWAUKEE, WI 53213

# Preparatory Exercises

### for acquiring
### the greatest possible independence and
### evenness of the fingers

ALOYS SCHMITT. Op. 16

Repeat each Exercise at least ten or twenty times, but omit the closing note until the final repetition. At first, practise each hand separately, then both together, always keeping the hands steady and quiet. Practise each Exercise slowly at first; increase the tempo gradually as the fingers acquire the necessary strength and flexibility.

It is advisable to practise these Exercises in the keys and without changing the fingering.

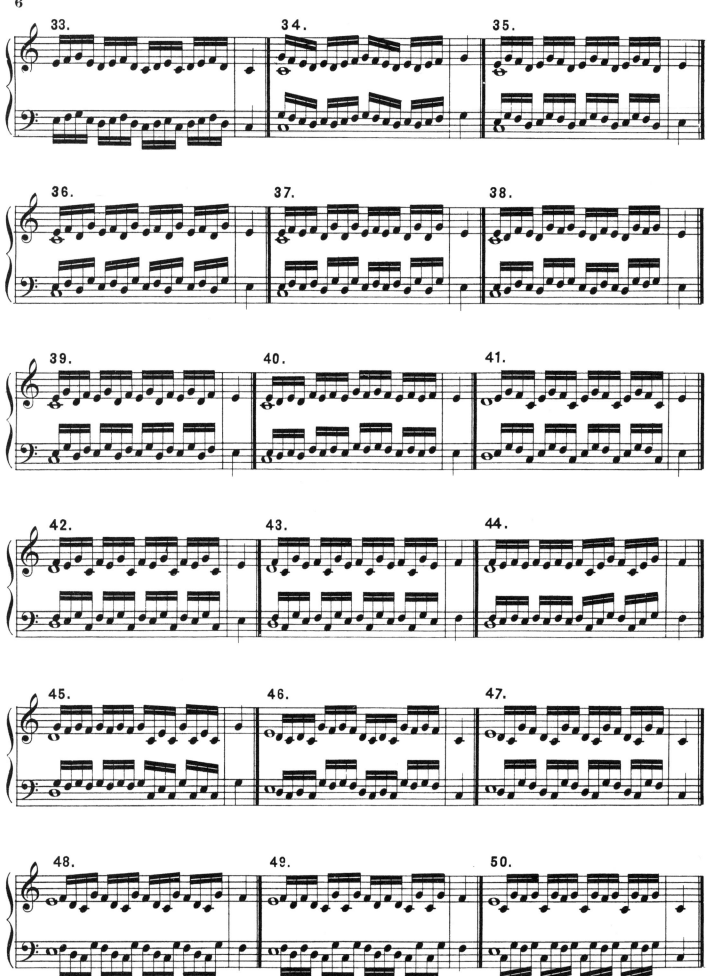

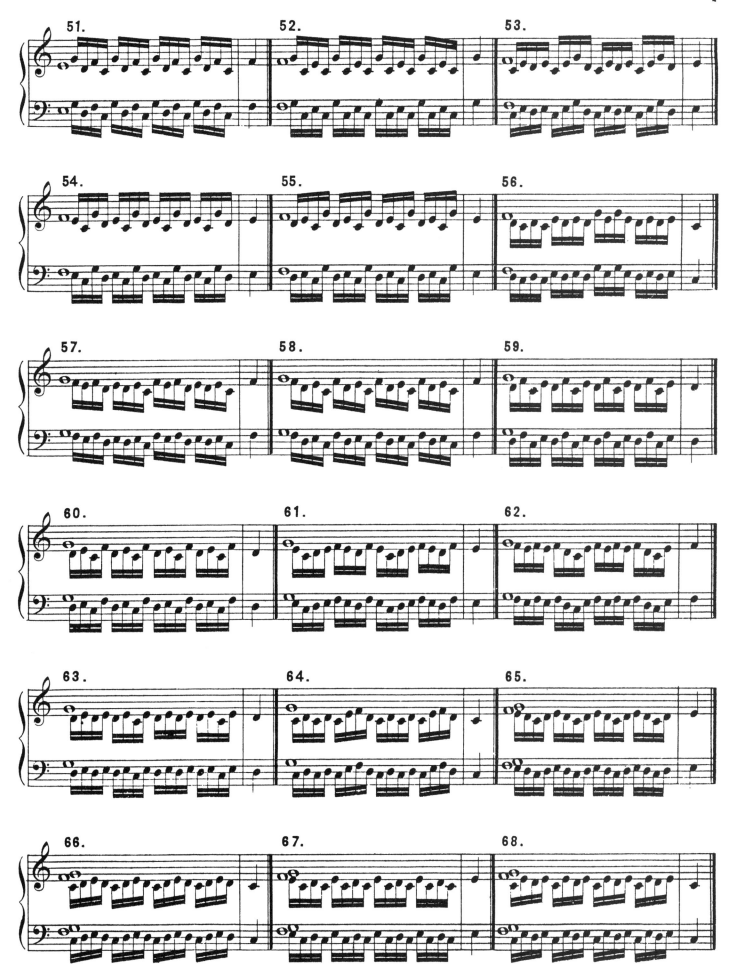

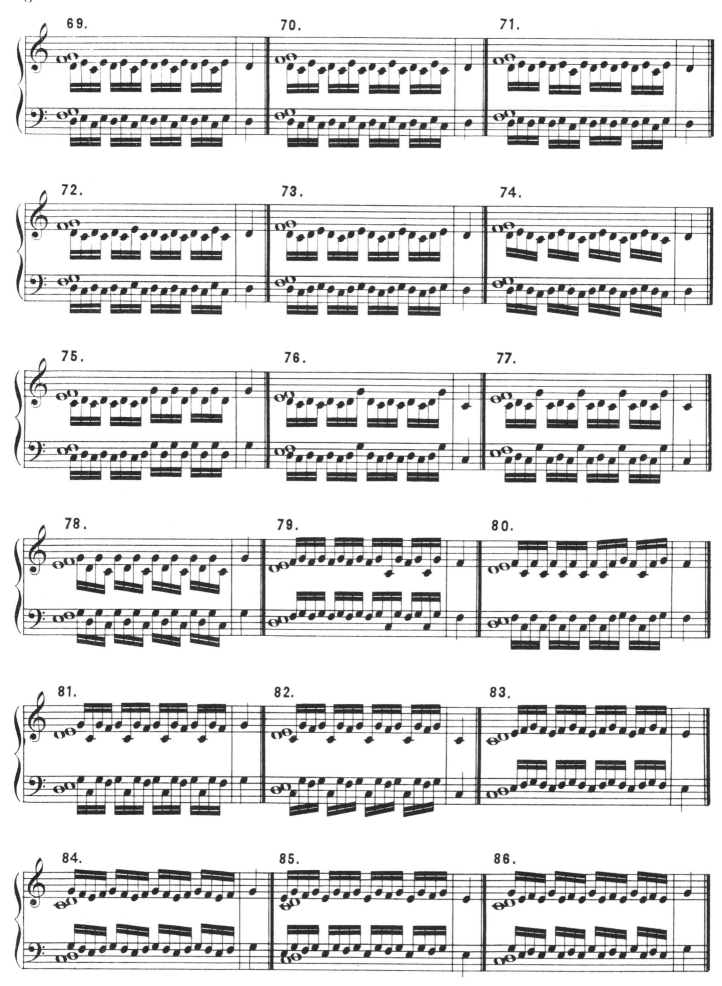

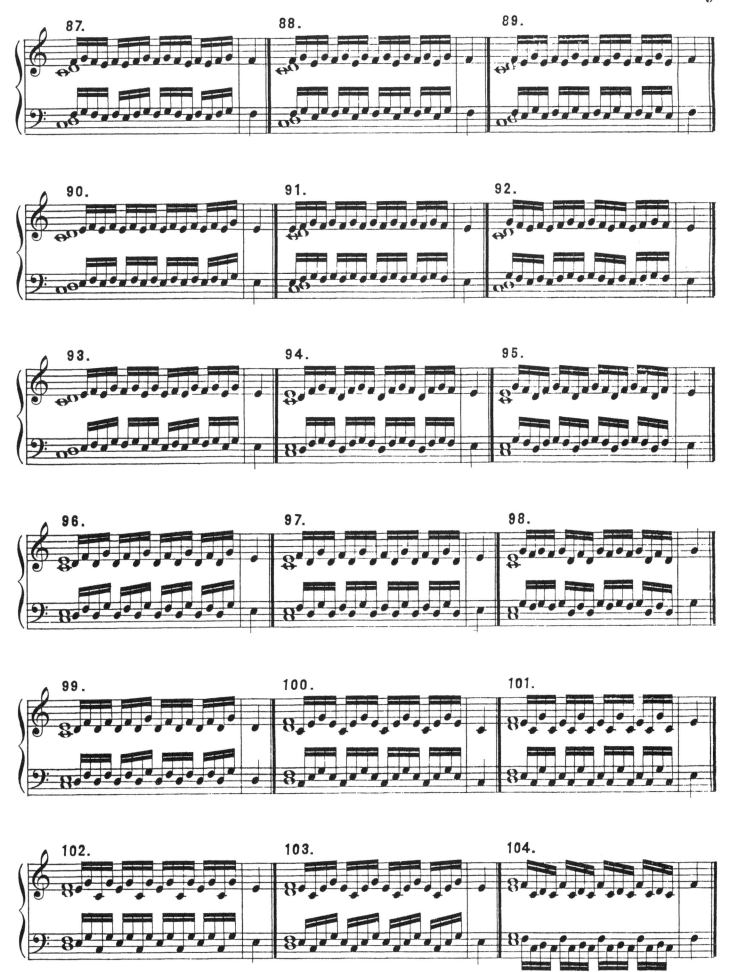

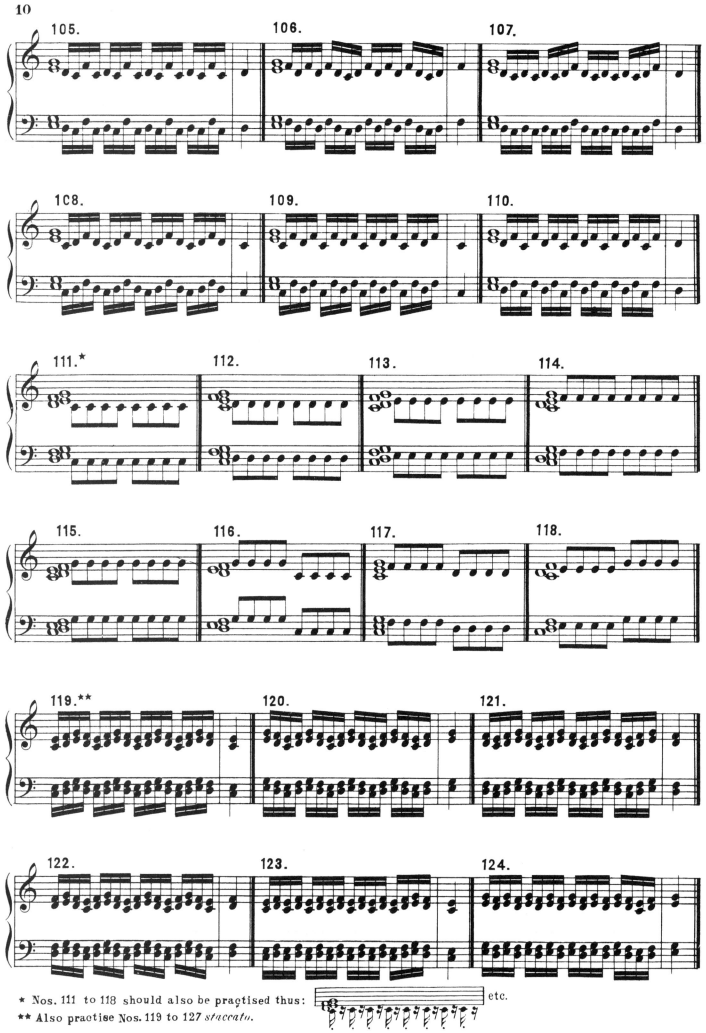

★ Nos. 111 to 118 should also be practised thus: etc.

★★ Also practise Nos. 119 to 127 *staccato*.

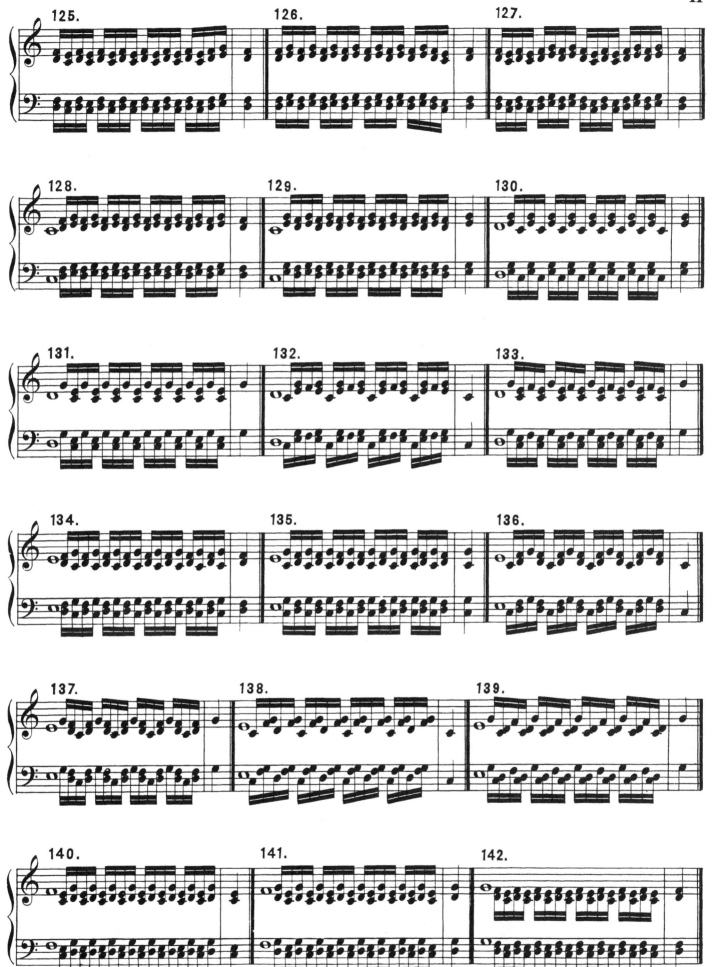

11

★ Nos. 160 to 169 should be played thus: etc.

These Exercises must be played, ascending and descending, the whole extent of the keyboard.

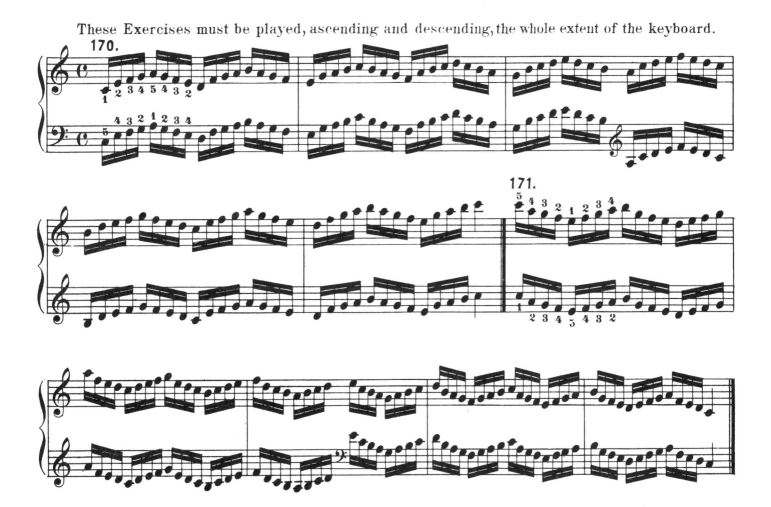

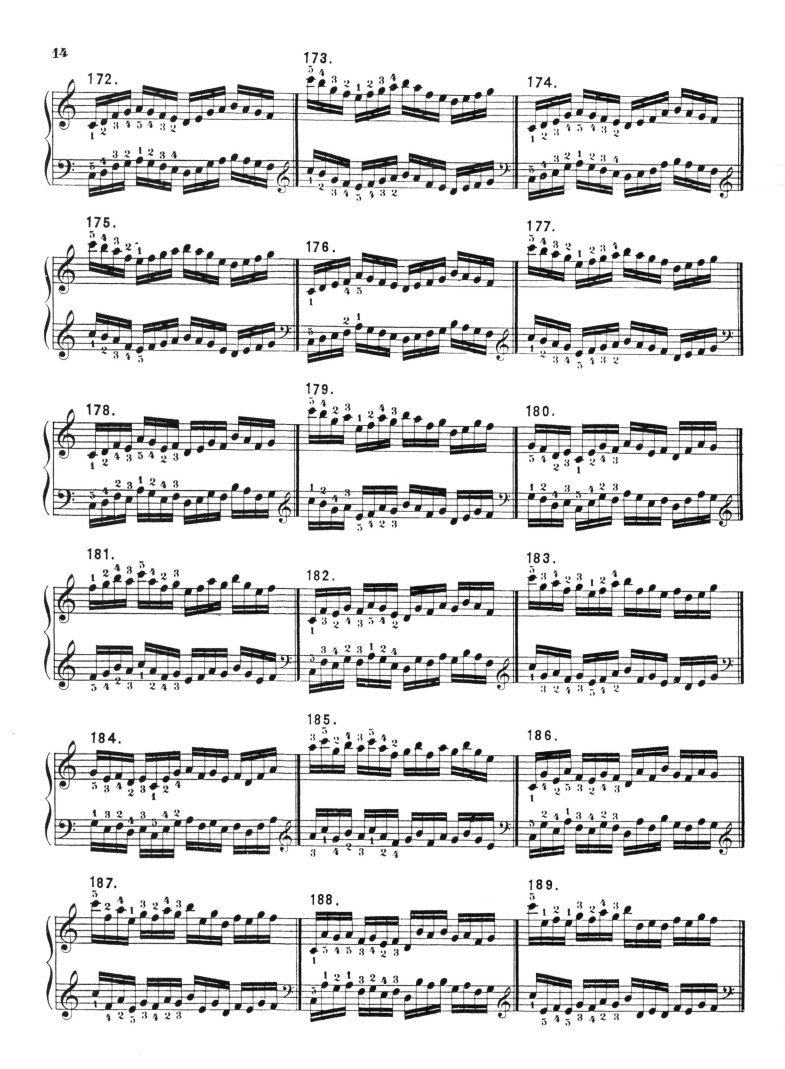

# Exercises

For passing the thumb under the fingers, preparatory to the practice of the
Scales and Arpeggios.

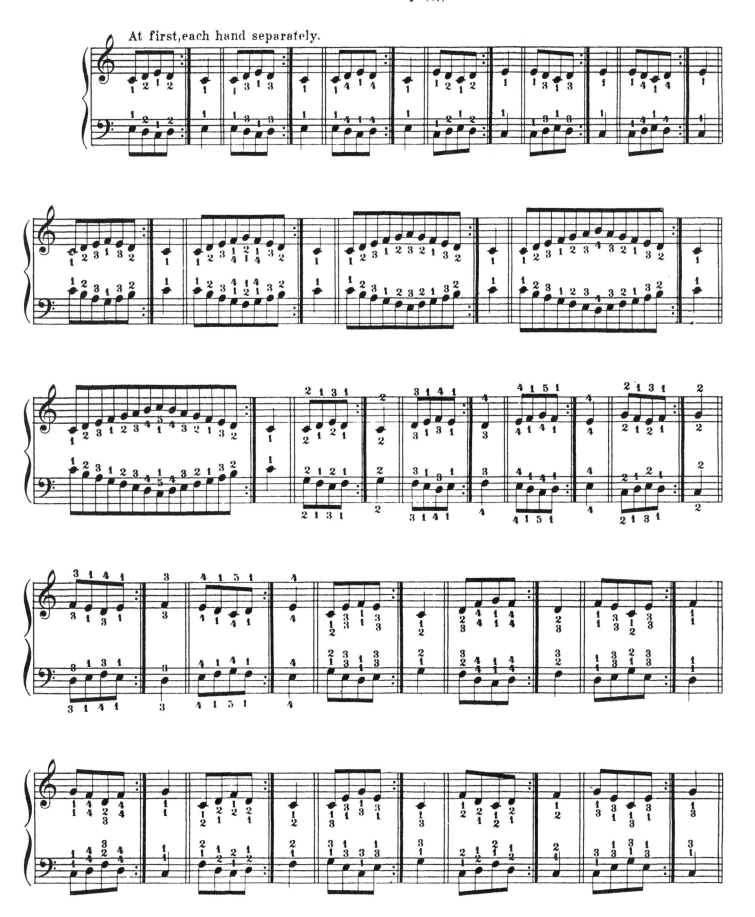

Each hand alone.
Right Hand.

Left Hand.

# Appendix

## Major Scales

A. Knecht

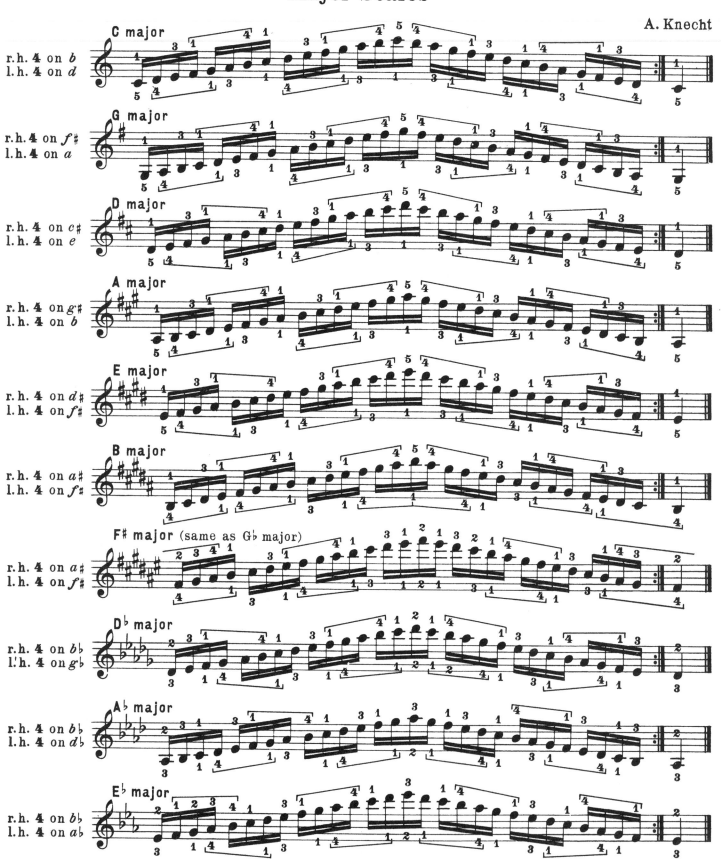

**N.B.** In the scales of *B, F♯, D♭, F major* and *B, E♭, B♭, F minor*, the thumbs of both hands fall on the same keys.

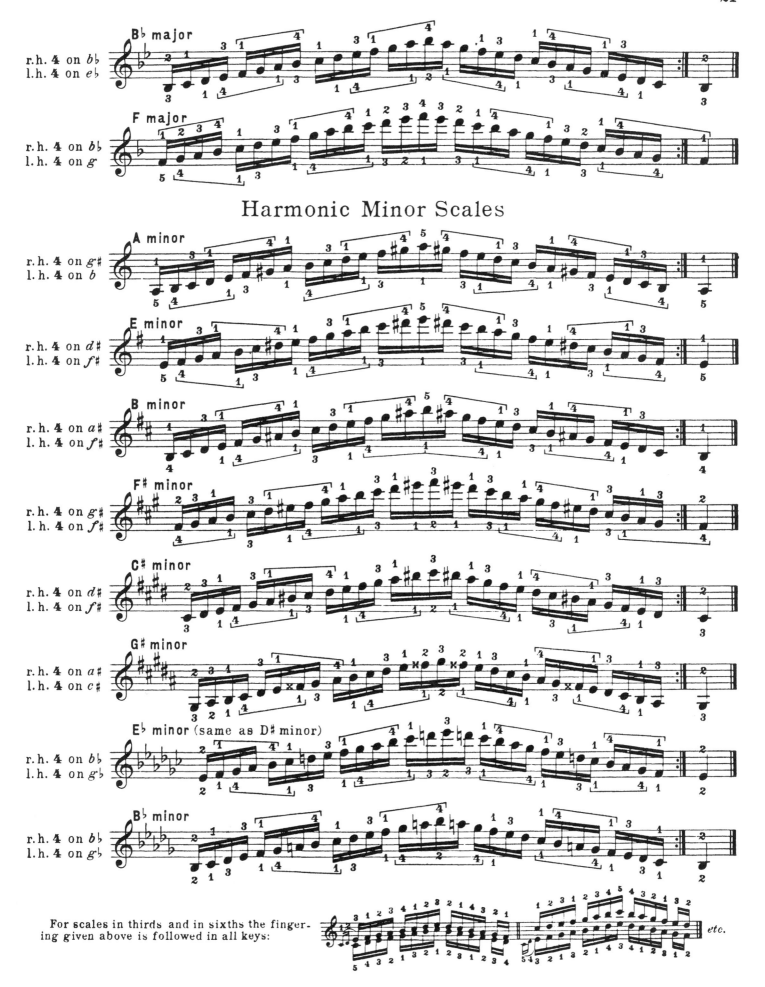

## Harmonic Minor Scales

For scales in thirds and in sixths the fingering given above is followed in all keys:

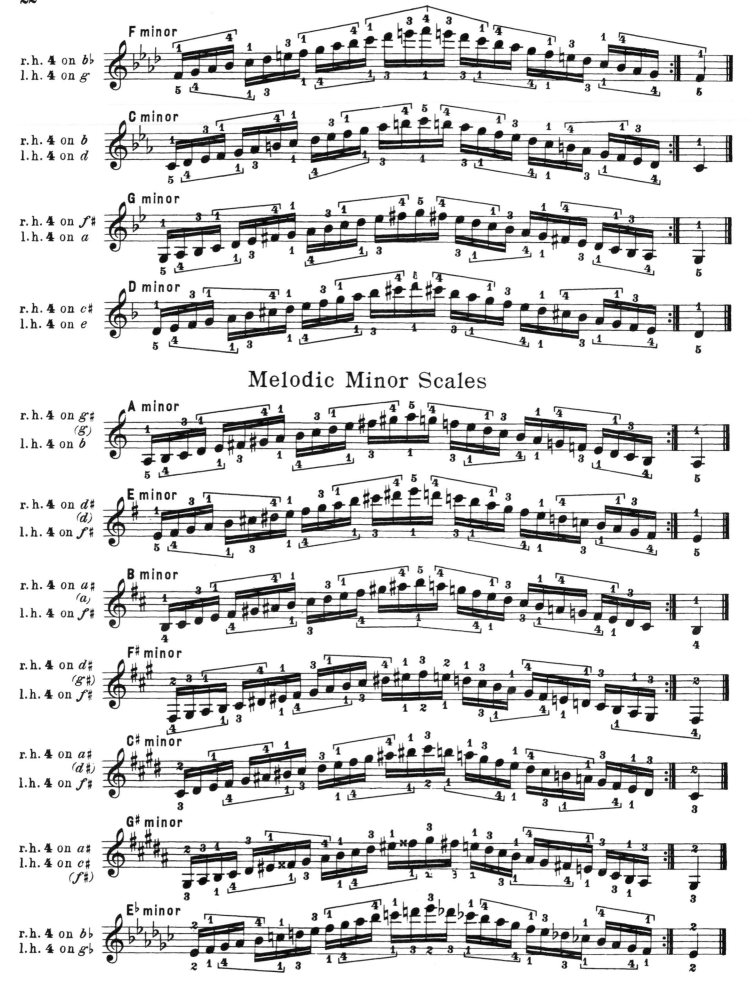

## Melodic Minor Scales

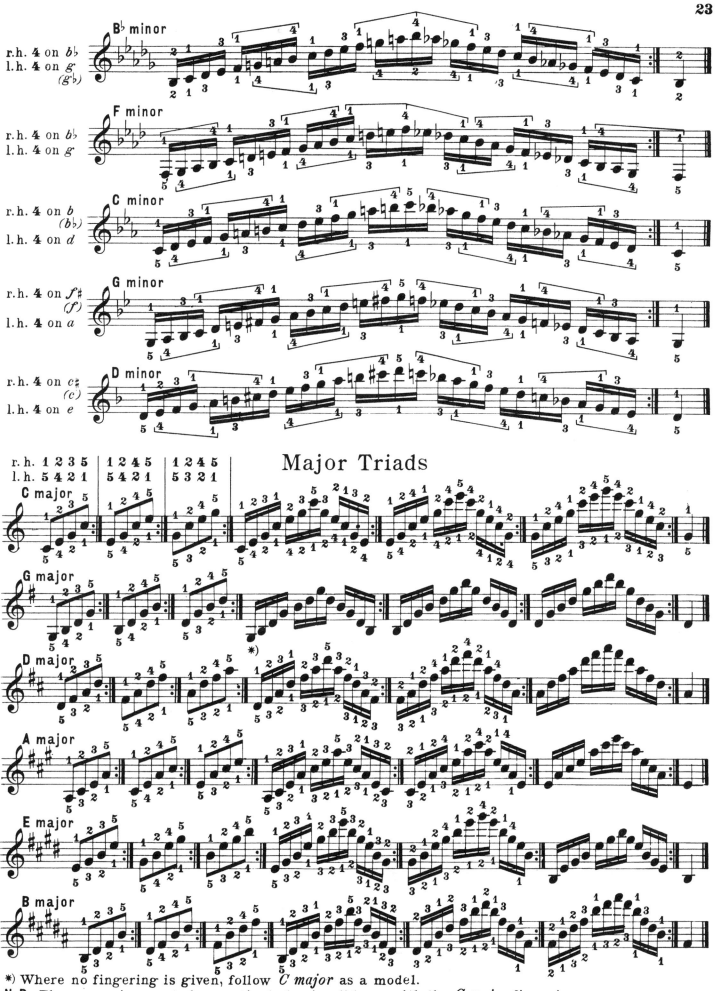

## Major Triads

*) Where no fingering is given, follow *C major* as a model.

**N.B.** The arpeggios are to be practiced also in all keys with the *C major* fingering.

Minor Triads

*) Where no fingering is given, follow *A minor* as a model.

## Dominant Seventh-Chords

**1.** To be played up and down through **3** octaves:

**2.** To be played as broken chords, like *C* and *G major,* with the same fingering in all chords:

Chromatic Scale

* Fingering *c* is not repeated until the third octave. The fingerings *a* and *b* are the same in every octave.

# Chord Passages

These Chord Passages have the same fingering in all keys.

# Scales in Double Thirds

**N.B.** The same fingering is repeated through each additional octave.

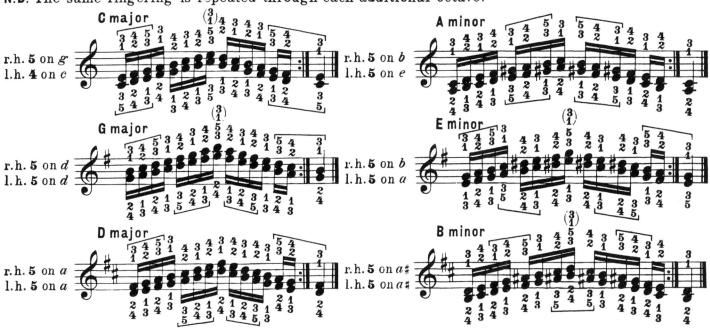

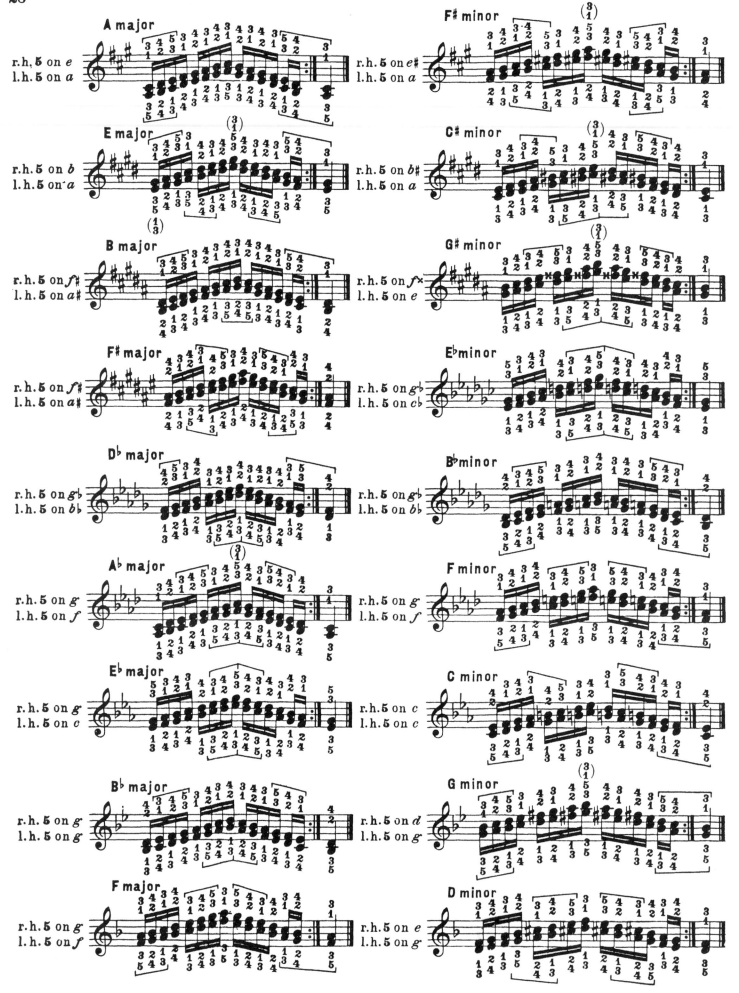

# Chromatic Scale in Double Minor Thirds

**N.B.** The same fingering is repeated through each additional octave.

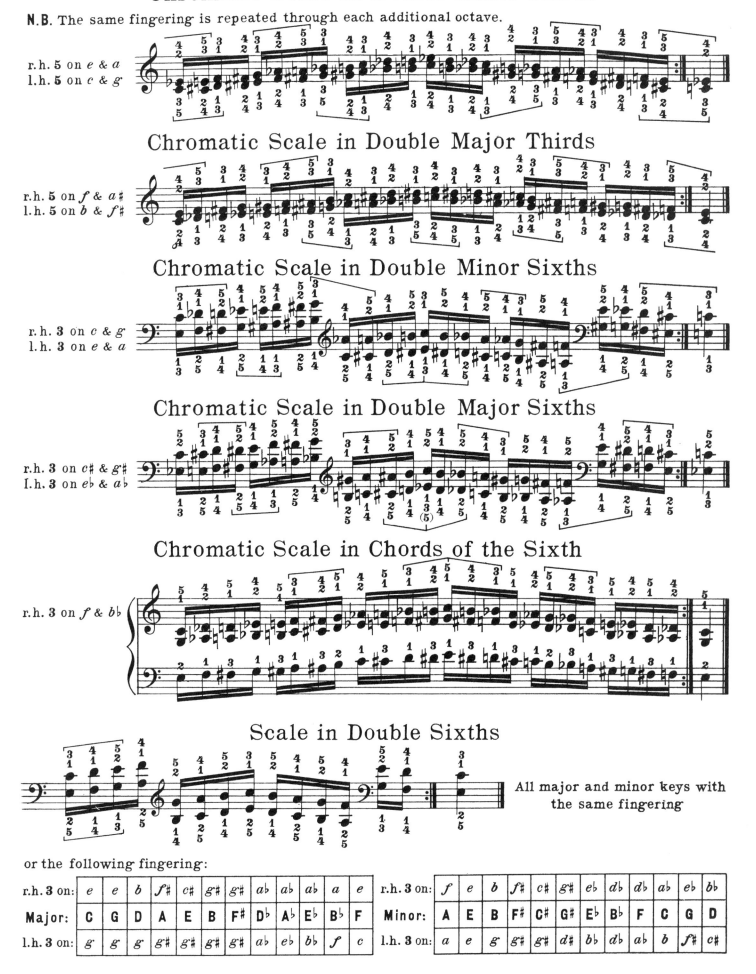

# Chromatic Scale in Double Major Thirds

# Chromatic Scale in Double Minor Sixths

# Chromatic Scale in Double Major Sixths

# Chromatic Scale in Chords of the Sixth

# Scale in Double Sixths

All major and minor keys with the same fingering

or the following fingering:

| r.h. 3 on: | e | e | b | f♯ | c♯ | g♯ | g♯ | ab | ab | ab | a | e |
|---|---|---|---|---|---|---|---|---|---|---|---|---|
| **Major:** | C | G | D | A | E | B | F♯ | D♭ | A♭ | E♭ | B♭ | F |
| l.h. 3 on: | g | g | g | g♯ | g♯ | g♯ | g♯ | ab | eb | bb | f | c |

| r.h. 3 on: | f | e | b | f♯ | c♯ | g♯ | eb | db | db | ab | eb | bb |
|---|---|---|---|---|---|---|---|---|---|---|---|---|
| **Minor:** | A | E | B | F♯ | C♯ | G♯ | E♭ | B♭ | F | C | G | D |
| l.h. 3 on: | a | e | g | g♯ | g♯ | d♯ | bb | db | ab | b | f♯ | c♯ |